discovermore

Transportation

Focus on Spacecraft

Doug Bradley

Britannica Educational Publishing

IN ASSOCIATION WITH

THE ROSEN PUBLISHING GROUP

Published in 2026 by Britannica Educational Publishing (a trademark of Encyclopædia Britannica, Inc.)
in association with The Rosen Publishing Group, Inc.
2544 Clinton Street, Buffalo, NY 14224

Distributed exclusively by Rosen Publishing.
To see additional Britannica Educational Publishing titles, go to rosenpublishing.com.

Editor: Greg Roza
Book Design: Michael Flynn

Photo Credits: Cover, pp. 5, 7 (bottom) Dima Zel/Shutterstock.com; (series background) Dai Yim/Shutterstock.com; p. 4 https://commons.wikimedia.org/wiki/File:Justus_Sustermans_-_Portrait_of_Galileo_Galilei,_1636.jpg; p. 7 (top) Johan Swanepoel/Shutterstock.com; p. 8 Hamara/Shutterstock.com; p. 9 VectorMine/Shutterstock.com; p. 10 https://commons.wikimedia.org/wiki/File:Dr._Robert_H._Goddard_-_GPN-2002-000131.jpg; p. 11 Paopano/Shutterstock.com; p. 12 agsaz/Shutterstock.com; p. 13 aapsky/Shutterstock.com; p. 14 JE Dean/Shutterstock.com; p. 15 Detyukov Sergey/Shutterstock.com; p. 16 Everett Collection/Shutterstock.com; p. 17 https://commons.wikimedia.org/wiki/File:Ed_White_with_Space_Gun_maneuvering_unit.jpg; p. 18 https://commons.wikimedia.org/wiki/File:Apollo_11_Lunar_Lander_-_5927_NASA.jpg; p. 19 https://commons.wikimedia.org/wiki/File:Buzz_salutes_the_U.S._Flag.jpg; p. 20 Dotted Yeti/Shutterstock.com; p. 21 joshimerbin/Shutterstock.com; p. 22 https://commons.wikimedia.org/wiki/File:Mars_Viking_11d128.png; p. 23 Triff/Shutterstock.com; p. 24 https://en.wikipedia.org/wiki/File:Space_Shuttle_Columbia_launching.jpg https://en.wikipedia.org/wiki/File:Space_Shuttle_Columbia_launching.jpg; p. 25 https://commons.wikimedia.org/wiki/File:Atlantis_silhouette.jpg; p. 27 (top) Rawpixel.com/Shutterstock.com; p. 27 (bottom) https://en.wikipedia.org/wiki/File:STS-116_spacewalk_1.jpg; p. 28 Jbruiz/Shutterstock.com; p. 29 3000ad/Shutterstock.com.

Cataloging-in-Publication Data

Names: Bradley, Doug, 1971-.
Title: Focus on spacecraft / Doug Bradley.
Description: New York : Britannica Educational Publishing, in association with Rosen Educational Services, 2026. | Series: Discover more: transportation | Includes glossary and index.
Identifiers: ISBN 9781641905541 (library bound) | ISBN 9781641905534 (pbk) | ISBN 9781641905558 (ebook)
Subjects: LCSH: Space vehicles--Juvenile literature. | Roving vehicles (Astronautics)--Juvenile literature.
Classification: LCC TL795.B697 2026 | DDC 629.47--dc23

Manufactured in the United States of America

Contents

Exploring Space

For thousands of years, even before the start of recordkeeping, humans have been fascinated by space. Starting in about 1600, scientists used telescopes to get a better view of the objects in the sky. Only in recent decades has it been possible to travel into space to get a closer look at the moon and other bodies.

In 1609, Italian scientist Galileo Galilei improved upon the earlier telescope designs. His telescope allowed him to discover the four largest moons of Jupiter, among other things.

The Earth's gravity is enough to keep the moon in orbit around it.

compare**and**contrast

An object's gravity depends on the amount of mass it has, which is the matter that makes up an object. What would life be like on Earth if the planet was half the size that it is now? What if the Earth was twice it's size?

A spaceship in orbit around the Earth is constantly falling. That's why astronauts experience weightlessness. However, the ship has reached a velocity that matches the force of gravity, resulting in a curved path around the planet.

Blast Off

The first rockets were used for fireworks and weapons. In the 1800s people began to think that rockets could be used to launch spacecraft as well.

Rockets carry fuel that is burned inside a chamber. The fuel can be either solid or liquid. The fuel burns when it is mixed with oxygen gas and ignited, or set on fire. As the fuel burns, it gives off a jet of hot gas that shoots out from an opening at the back of the chamber. The force of the gas moving backward pushes the rocket forward. This action is called jet **propulsion**.

Rockets are needed to launch spaceships into outer space.

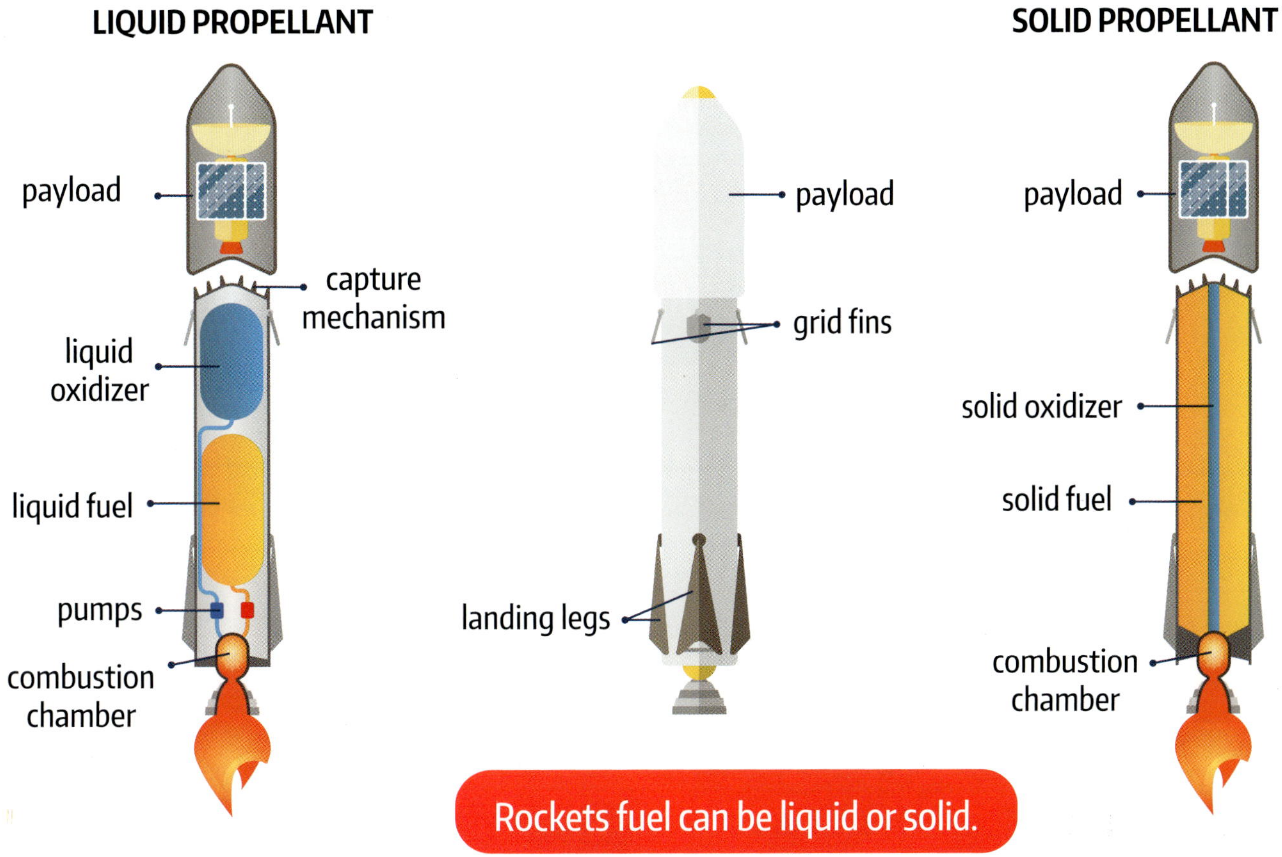

The engines of a jet airplane work in a similar way to rockets. But jet engines get their oxygen from the air. However, there's no oxygen in outer space, so rockets must carry their own oxygen supply.

WORD WISE

PROPULSION MEANS THE ACTION OF PROPELLING OR PUSHING FORWARD. PROPULSION IS WHAT ALLOWS ROCKETS TO GET TO THE RIGHT SPEED TO ACHIEVE ORBIT AROUND EARTH.

In 1926, American scientist Robert Goddard launched the first liquid-fueled rocket from his aunt's farm in Auburn, Massachusetts. In the 1930s and 1940s people worked on making rockets more powerful. Many rockets were used as weapons during World War II (1939–45).

Today, Goddard is called the father of modern rocketry. Without his advances, space travel would not be possible.

This is an illustration of a space shuttle in orbit around Earth.

In the 1950s scientists began to develop rockets to use for spacecraft. It takes a great deal of power to reach the required speed of at least 25,000 miles (40,000 km) per hour to escape Earth's gravity. The rockets that launch spacecraft are therefore very large. The Saturn V rocket built in the 1960s was 363 feet (111 m) tall. Today's spacecraft may use more than one type of rocket. One type may be used to launch the spacecraft and another to move it around once it is on its way. The space shuttle, shown here, was a vehicle that was launched into space by rockets but then landed like an airplane when it returned.

Consider This

Most of the fuel in a rocket is used in the first few minutes of a flight. Why do you think this is?

A Sky Full of Satellites

Humans have launched many satellites into orbit since the development of rockets. A satellite is a small object that orbits a larger object in space. Satellites can be natural or artificial (made by people). The moon is a natural satellite of Earth. Artificial satellites are sent into space to gather information. Most are launched into space by rockets.

This replica, or copy, of Sputnik 1 is in the Museum of Space and Missile Technology, Saint Petersburg, Russia.

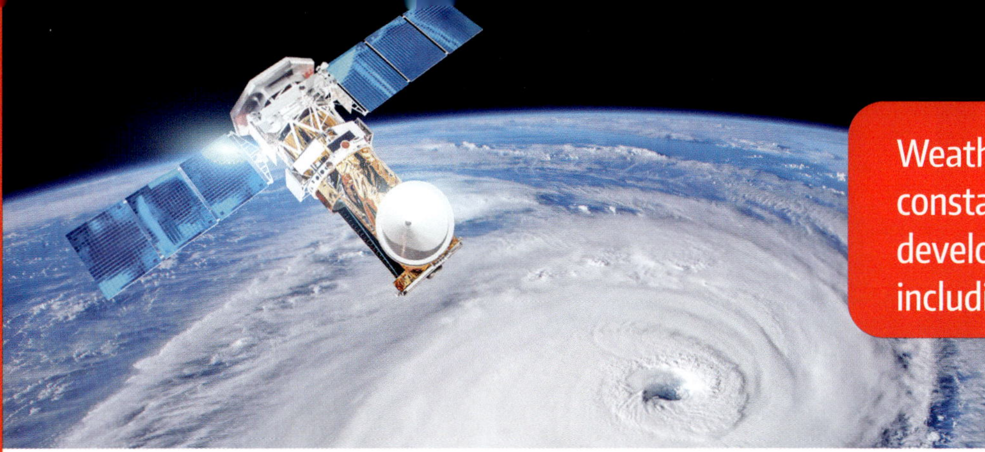

Weather satellites keep constant watch on weather developments on Earth, including hurricanes.

The first artificial satellite was Sputnik 1. The Soviet Union launched Sputnik into orbit around Earth in 1957. The first successful U.S. satellite was Explorer 1, which was launched in 1958. Now dozens of new satellites are put into space every year.

Scientific satellites collect information about space. Communications satellites help send telephone calls, radio and television programs, and computer information around the world. Satellites are used in weather forecasting. Militaries use satellites for spying. Airplanes, ships, and cars can use information from satellites to find the way from place to place.

Consider This

As of 2025, there are about 11,700 man-made satellites orbiting Earth! Hundreds of older satellites have been moved to the "graveyard orbit," also called the "junk orbit," that is farther away from Earth. Why do you think this is important?

The Race to Space

The United States increased its space research after the Soviet Union launched Sputnik 1. Both the United States and the Soviet Union wanted to be the first nation to put a person in space. This became known as the Space Race.

The National Aeronautics and Space Administration (NASA) took charge of the U.S. effort. NASA began Project Mercury in 1958. The goals were to put a spacecraft in orbit with a man onboard, to see how a human could function in space, and to return the man and spacecraft safely.

The Freedom 7 capsule, shown here, was the first U.S. manned spacecraft to reach space.

Gagarin was given the title of Hero of the Soviet Union for his trip into space. Many monuments were put up to celebrate his achievements.

The Soviet Union was the first country to send a human into space. The **cosmonaut** Yuri Gagarin flew a single orbit around Earth aboard Vostok 1 on April 12, 1961. Shortly after that, on May 5, 1961, astronaut Alan B. Shepard, Jr., became the first American to enter space. Shepard flew for only 15 minutes and did not complete an orbit around Earth.

WORD WISE

COSMONAUT IS THE RUSSIAN WORD FOR ASTRONAUT. THIS WORD COMES FROM THE RUSSIAN WORDS FOR "UNIVERSE" AND "SAILOR."

Let's Take a Spacewalk!

Shortly after Gagarin's trip to space, the United States successfully sent a man into space and returned him safely. The follow-up, Project Gemini, was announced in January 1962. The goal was to learn even more about how humans can function and survive in space for longer periods of time. It also allowed astronauts to learn how to control a spacecraft in flight.

This photograph of the Gemini 6 orbiter was taken from the Gemini 7 orbiter in December 1965.

On June 3, 1965, Ed White became the first American to perform a spacewalk.

The Gemini spacecraft had room for two astronauts. Its missions helped scientists learn how astronauts could travel outside a spacecraft in a spacesuit. They also learned how to connect two spacecraft together in space.

The first manned Gemini flight was Gemini 3 on March 23, 1965. Virgil I. Grissom and John W. Young completed three orbits of Earth. During the flight of Gemini 4, later in 1965, Edward H. White II became the first American to walk in space, although it was more floating than walking.

Consider This

The cord attached to White in the photograph is also attached to the spaceship during the Gemini 4 mission. Why do you think this was necessary?

On the Moon

From 1961 to 1975, Project Apollo accomplished 11 spaceflights. The Apollo astronauts rode in a section called the command module. The Apollo spacecraft was larger than the spacecraft previously used for the Mercury and Gemini programs.

Today, you can see the Apollo command module up close at the Kennedy Space Center in Merritt Island, Florida.

Astronaut Buzz Aldrin planted the American flag on the moon before making the return trip to Earth.

On July 16, 1969, Neil Armstrong, Edwin E. (Buzz) Aldrin, Jr., and Michael Collins left for the moon on the Apollo 11 mission. Four days later, Armstrong and Aldrin moved from the command module to a smaller vehicle called the lunar module. The lunar module, also called the Eagle, then separated from the rest of the craft. Armstrong and Aldrin flew the Eagle to the surface of the moon. Armstrong became the first person to step onto the moon. For more than two hours Armstrong and Aldrin collected samples of moon rocks and soil, made measurements, and took photographs.

Consider This

Why do you think the Apollo astronauts brought rock and soil samples back from the moon?

Deep Space

In order to study deep space, scientists have created space probes. These are vehicles that carry scientific equipment but no passengers. Some make one-way voyages into deep space. The probes that did not land on planets or other bodies are still traveling through space. Probes are controlled from Earth by radio. They send back their findings the same way. The probes gather pictures and other information about planets and distant parts of the solar system.

Two interstellar probes, Voyager 1 and Voyager 2, were launched in 1977. They flew by planets on the way to the edge of the solar system. They are still flying away from Earth, and will continue to do so forever!

NASA launched the Europa Clipper in October 2024. This probe will reach Europa, one of Jupiter's moons, in April 2030. Scientists have long wanted to study this moon up close.

In the late 1950s the Soviet Union and the United States launched their first deep-space probes. Probes eventually landed on the planets Mars and Venus and flew past the planets Jupiter, Saturn, Uranus, and Neptune. They collected information on the planets' atmospheres, moons, and ring systems. In the early 2000s scientists sent several new probes to explore Mars and other planets and objects in space.

Consider This

What kind of information do you think probes collect when they fly past a planet or a moon? What do you think scientists hope to discover on Europa?

Landing on Mars

A spacecraft made to rest on the surface of a planet or other body in space is called a lander. A rover is a lander that can move around. They gather information about the planet and send the information back to Earth.

Several landers have been sent to the surface of Mars in order to explore the planet more closely. In 1975 Viking 1 was the first American spacecraft to touch the surface of Mars. It was also the first spacecraft ever to remain there. It followed a series of short-lived Soviet probes that either landed or crashed into the surface.

NASA's Viking Mission was the first to successfully put a lander on Mars. The Viking 1 lander took the first close-up photographs of the Red Planet's surface.

By 2020, a total of 21 landers had attempted to land on the surface of Mars, although some failed to. As of 2025, two rovers were still actively exploring Mars: the Curiosity rover and Perseverance rover.

It is difficult to land a probe on the surface of a planet safely. The Mars Exploration Rovers (which landed in 2004) were protected by large airbags. The airbags provided a softer landing by making them a bit like large bouncing balls.

Consider This

Mars is an average of 140 million miles (225 million km) away from Earth. How long do you think it would take to travel there?

Reusable Spacecraft

NASA launched the first space shuttle in 1981. This is a type of reusable spacecraft. The main section had wings and was called the orbiter. Attached to the orbiter were rockets, fuel tanks, and oxygen tanks. These boosted the craft through the thickest part of Earth's atmosphere. The shuttles had space for as many as seven astronauts to live and work. They also had a large cargo area. At the end of a mission, the orbiter returned to Earth and landed like an airplane.

The first shuttle, Columbia, was first launched on April 12, 1981. Columbia's last flight launched on February 1, 2003.

The last space shuttle, the Atlantis, can be seen here as it passes in front of the sun!

There were five shuttles altogether, but two of them were destroyed in accidents. They made more than 100 flights between 1981 and 2011. Each flight lasted up to about two weeks. The astronauts brought supplies to other spacecraft, repaired satellites, performed experiments, and helped build the International Space Station. The last shuttle mission, in 2011, was the 135th mission for the Space Shuttle program.

Consider This

On June 18, 1983, astronaut Sally Ride became the first American woman in space. As of 2025, 55 other female American astronauts have followed in Ride's footsteps.

An International Mission

A spacecraft that remains in a fixed orbit around Earth for an extended period of time is called a space station. Astronauts can live on a space station for months at a time to gather scientific data and conduct experiments. The Soviets launched the world's first space station, Salyut 1, on April 19, 1971. The United States launched its first space station, Skylab, on May 14, 1973. It lasted six years.

In the 1990s several countries worked together to design and build the International Space Station (ISS). The first part of the space station was placed in orbit in 1998. Other parts were added later. Astronauts from many countries now take turns living and working on the ISS.

In space travel the effects of gravity are not felt as they are on Earth. Anything that is not tied down will float around a spacecraft. Those who live on the ISS have to learn how to move through the craft, and they sleep in bags that are mounted on the wall.

Skylab was manned between May 1973 and February 1974. In July 1979, the spaceship was allowed to crash into the Indian Ocean.

compare and contrast

How do you think life is different for astronauts living on the International Space Station? How long do you think you could make it aboard the ISS?

As of the writing of this book, more than 270 astronauts from around the world have lived and worked on the International Space Station.

Where to Next?

The research being done on the International Space Station and in other locations is helping scientists understand what they need to do to send humans into other parts of outer space. The locations scientists are preparing to explore with spacecraft include the moon, Mars, Mercury, Europa, and several **asteroids**.

NASA's DART probe was purposely crashed into an asteroid in September 2022! Scientists are searching for ways to deflect, or send away, asteroids approaching Earth.

This is an artist's representation of what a science facitlity would look like on the surface of Mars.

Eventually, NASA hopes to send human missions to Mars. Many things must be accomplished for that to become a possibility. Mars is very far away from Earth. A trip to the planet would take years. Scientists do not know if humans can live that long in space. However, scientists have learned a lot from working on the International Space Station and other spacecraft. They have also learned a great deal about Mars from the Mars rovers. However, it's just a matter of time before humans themselves walk on the surface of the Red Planet!

WORD WISE

AN ASTEROID IS A SMALL, ROCKY BODY THAT ORBITS THE SUN.

Glossary

astronaut A person who travels in a spacecraft.
atmosphere A layer of gases that surrounds a planet.
data Facts that are collected and studied.
deep space Space outside Earth's atmosphere and especially that part lying beyond the Earth-moon system.
experiment A procedure or operation carried out under controlled conditions in order to discover something, to test a hypothesis, or to serve as an example.
exploration The act of investigating an unknown area.
interstellar Located or taking place among or between the stars.
launch To send off an object, especially with force.
NASA The National Aeronautics and Space Administration, the space agency of the United States.
orbit The path taken by one body circling around another body.
probe An unmanned spacecraft that explores objects in space and transmits data back to Earth.
rover A space vehicle built to move across the surface of a planet or other body in space.
satellite A small object that orbits a larger object in space.
solar system A star with the group of heavenly bodies that revolve around it.
space The region beyond Earth's atmosphere.
space station A spacecraft in a fixed orbit around Earth.
spacesuit A special suit designed to allow an astronaut to survive in space.
spacewalk Any physical movement of an astronaut outside a spacecraft in space.
tether A line by which something is fastened so as to limit its range.
velocity The rate of change of position along a straight line with respect to time.

For More Information

Books

DK staff. *Behind the Scenes at the Space Station*. London, UK: DK Children, 2022.

Morgan, Elizabeth. *Is Exploring Space Important?* Buffalo, NY: KidHaven Publishing, 2024.

Websites

International Space Station
www.nasa.gov/international-space-station
Learn a lot more about the ISS from NASA.

Mars Facts
science.nasa.gov/mars/facts
Read all about Mars here and find links to other Mars information.

Publisher's note to educators and parents: Our editors have carefully reviewed these websites to ensure that they are suitable for students. Many websites change frequently, however, and we cannot guarantee that a site's future contents will continue to meet our high standards of quality and educational value. Be advised that students should be closely supervised whenever they access the internet.

Index